THE ID KID

The Id Kid

Linda Besner

SIGNAL EDITIONS IS AN IMPRINT OF VÉHICULE PRESS

Published with the generous assistance of The Canada Council for the
Arts, the Canada Book Fund of the Department of Canadian Heritage,
and the Société de développement des entreprises culturelles du Québec
(SODEC).

SIGNAL EDITIONS EDITOR: CARMINE STARNINO

Cover design: David Drummond
Photo of author: Adrienne Gruber
Set in Minion by Simon Garamond
Printed by Marquis Book Printing Inc.

LIBRARY AND ARCHIVES CANADA CATALOGUING IN PUBLICATION

Besner, Linda
The id kid / Linda Besner, 1980-

. Poems.
ISBN 978-1-55065-313-7

I. Title.

PS8603.E7745I45 2011   C811'.6   C2011-901218-9

Published by Véhicule Press, Montréal, Québec, Canada
www.vehiculepress.com

Distribution in Canada by LitDistCo
orders@litdistco.ca
Distributed in the U.S. by Independent Publishers Group
www.ipgbook.com

Printed in Canada on 100% post-consumer recycled paper.

*for Rae Brown
of Pugwash, Nova Scotia*

Contents

iv. Courtly Love

v. Thumbwars

THE DEVIL: You're a very bad man.
BOBBY GOULD: Nothing's black and white.
THE DEVIL: Nothing's black and white, nothing's black and white—
what about a panda? What about a panda, you dumb fuck!
What about a fucking panda!

—*Bobby Gould in Hell*, David Mamet

I

Knick Knack

Umbrella

The blueprints promised an introvert:
rain-stammered dotted lines. Pleat
here, punch out
into bell-shaped firmament,
collapsible blue idea.

Featherweights of human ingenuity
tricked out in canvas, oilcloth,
a springloaded halo of interiority
tossed aloft with fanfare, or a private click.

All so deftly spiked by a minor change of wind's
leaping brilliancies.

> Nineteen oh five and three inventors calf-deep
> in the Seine, preparing to tug by motorboat
> their newest flying machine,
> a float glider of flapping white boxes.
> *Ces merveilleux fous volants dans leurs drôles
> de machines...*
> Glorified kites,
> the earth duochrome and tilted: aileron,
> ornithopter. Sky key.

Instead, it's a blown disguise,
a daddy-long-legs on a steel leash,
a false statement, irretractable,

a mad plaid hope pedalling dastardly
towards its own destruction.

Aluminium spokes wheeling bravely into the storm.

Better luck next time, boys.
Another bright idea gone tits-up into the ditch.

Moonlight on Komatsu Excavator

-after *A Streetcar Named Desire*

Honey, this streetlight's a dash of cold water in the face—
but it won't wake you.

                          Who's gone off and left you like this in the dark?
That orange steel forehead slumped on the tarmac,
gravel scattered like cards you've dropped face up.
                                        A smashed rum bottle
                                        by your joisted cheek.

Looks like you're all powered down to zero,
                          those rubber-tube muscles hanging slack.

If I glimmer right up close, sugar, I can see
straight into that tinted glass box in your reinforced chest—

AM radio, ashtray with the lighter built in, joystick, oh my—
but looks like there's no one in the driver's seat.

That boxy body,
treaded for traction—you roll right over it all,
never spare a sensation for what you've crushed.

You've almost got me
believing in oblivion—but not quite! Oh, not quite, honey!

For something playing possum, your shiny edges are trying awfully
hard to bounce me into the gutter. Tomorrow
you'll have to rev up, dig deeper.

                          You won't mind if I
lean on you in this off-the-shoulder white dress?
I feel a little faint when the clouds jostle through.

                You wouldn't be bothered by
a light finger of regret
drawn along your strong arm, dabbling
at the cold flat of your thigh?
                   Like you told me,
Some people seldom touch it, but it touches them often.

Discarded Chairs

–after *Death of a Salesman*

so this is what falls outta the magician's sleeve around here—
a construction site heap of willy lomans with the legs kicked off.

broken down old kids in duplicate, triplicate, christ
there's hundreds of you, all the same sorry shape

bent over sideways, down on one shoulder, face in the dirt.
backs pinned to the ground, open seats worn shiny.

looks like they gonna fix this place up, huh? poor chumps.
you're a shelf-full of size seven-and-a-halfs when the world

wears an eight. don't look at me like that. let me tell you something,
it was a long road through the pineal glands

of a barrel of monkeys to *cogito ergo sum*, digging inside the
cranium for something that glows. you don't got it.

don't tell me i *can't eat the orange and throw the peel away.*
a man is not a piece of fruit, but listen kids,

all the straight-backed near-misses in the world don't add up
to a hit; you're not canyon leapers,

you're a volley of badminton birds who fell just short of the net.
i can't unpick you from yourselves.

to hell with it. that big-jawed yellow bruiser
looks ready to rumble over here and mash you up.

i gotta stay on this side of the orange netting,
we're all flimsy enough as it is.

hey chin up, fellas; they've won, but they still can't see
that it hurts you. so long.

Demolition Site: AIDS, 1990

–after *Angels in America: A Gay Fantasia on National Themes*

PLASTIC SHEET:

Here I am, darling! The glad rag transparent. A shred
of sheer radiance stapled to the catwalk where I preen
and turn—liar! You love it!—in the ghostly wind,

waving to the work glove stuck in the muddy fence,
tame little social animal poised
to rip my throat out. Throw your roses now

if you can cram them through the grid,
the sneeze-guard. You're not suited up to touch me.
Where the sidewalk ends, *chérie*, is churning emptiness,

infected cavity of the universe. Look through me at the trench,
the grave, the snake-pit. Copperhead wire, pylon-nest,
the squeeze is on. Stare away; it's not every day

you see a whole street demolished. The ravaged rooms
of a block that *dies at thirty, robbed of decades of majesty.*
Trust me, sweet, there's no glory in this hole.

SCAFFOLD:

Shh, I'm hiding. Risen above, you see, except my baser instincts—
they've got me cruising hardhats. Wouldn't you love to follow one

into the little girls' room, that dusty blue haven breathing
1-88-TOILET-88. Shoot me to the moon, Rent-A-Can!

I'd invite you to stay a spell and watch, but you're already glued
to the chink in the chainmail fence. Fascinating, isn't it?

Morbidly so. I'm afraid of heights, but to be honest, more afraid
to be down there. I deserted; stretched to my moral extremity.

I'm an iron beanstalk espaliered against the strongest wall in sight.
My clinging will bring it to its knees, eventually.

Though broken sticks of braver structures shame the ground,
I'm yet untouched, free. Would it be too forward

if I...invited you up? I'm not as cold as I look.
You're scared. So am I. Everyone is in the land of the free.

PIT:

Keep staring, you cowards.
You dead-ends, you schmucks,
you losers, you nothings. Watch
and see: these are the rules of progress.
Wherever they claw up the foundation,
where the orange golems dig into rot,
when the big Cat rips in purring,
you will find me, always. Keep looking.
I have looked, I have searched all my life
for absolute bottom, and I found it, believe me.

CAUTION TAPE:

Get somewhere you can take off that shirt and throw it away,
and don't touch the blood.

SCAFFOLD:

I believe in the silver decks of justice, ascending planks
I can toe, or walk. Easy, at least, to find me here,

when judgment comes. And underneath, squiggles of burnt wire,
orange spray paint to number the depths of my fall—

T 3′ 2′ 1′—the levels glowing. Dismembered wristwatch,
coils and connectors sprinkled with lime.

If this is the end of days, the wilderness a granite garden,
if this is parable borne out in blowtorch and dynamite,

who left will be willing? To say for me,
yisgadal ve'yiskadash sh'mey rabo, sh'mey de kidshoh—

PLASTIC SHEET:

Snails' tails and sludgy bubblegum, the new tarmac's
getting laid, lucky thing. It has possibilities, this décor,
n'est-ce pas? Bolts of orange silk, bold blue-and-white

Tyvek moving in. I'm hanging on by spider-spit.
The dandelion heads orbiting the scragged edges
will see more of how the world turns out than I.

But maybe—just maybe—I'll be transformed.
A makeover. The crane stretches a white arm over 9th street,
esthetician angel with a chain bracelet dangling from her wrist.
No accidents. No regrets. *The Great Work begins.*

Wartime Puppet Play of the Kitchen Stove

To fight with bowl and arrow, mustard seed and gas. To the

Northeast the crockery clashed, tea-towels bannering while

Renegade kernels whistled dixie south of the Mason jar line.

Fallen to the foxhole basin drain the pierced sieve gurgling

Hundredfold to black. The peppermill lighthoused a warning:

GADZOOKS! Through five-alarm smoke, four raging bull's-eyes

Brayed from pea-green fields aflame to Oxo cubes penned in and

Bleating. Behind the wall, the voices of disembodied mice

Uplifted with the tin can resistance in their banned anthem,

La Mayonnaise.

In the fallout a scuttled Bialetti slept on the sandscuffed rim.

The demobbed double boiler, its cold helmet fogged yet with

Flashbacks of dead steam, huddled thinking: *For them; for their*

Thankless foppish freedom those nigger wop commie jews...

No warmth from the citadel where sickly butter hid.

In the pockmarked plain of the ashen range, the dusty dishrag

Wrung its black-and-white checks. Knelt alone repeating to the fan

Blowing the all clear, *La afham. La a'ref. La adri.*

(I don't understand. I don't know. I have no idea.)

Tennis Court

at midday struck with heat like a dinner gong,
                                      blueblood turned bluebottle,
a coup
of blackguard moss & worker ants profaning—what?
a deserted table where
the milk has been upset,
backcourt a pool
                          of curdled blue, the listless posts
stunned as empty tea-urns.
                          where bloodlusting mosquitoes nip
at unwinched handles that have lost their grip,
net's snappy victrola
                          wound down & gone;

all that's green isn't grass or at least not initially—
it had intention, this clearing:
                          once, pressed whites for the old gent,
                          boater hats, leisure suits, lemonade.
on the out-of-bounds line an earwiggish pair of leftover rackets:
one an unstrung mandolin,
                          the other a nonsense of shabby gridwork,
oval embroidery frame
its birds half-conjured
                          with the needle through the eye
back when a quarter-inch
          still meant something.

once it was in or it was out, one-love could sum it all up,
hit & run, run & swing,
                          ashes ashes we all fall prey
to the cottoncandy smell of dying fir,
                          flash of mica in the hot stones.
A sugarglass empire on which the sun has set,
clocked, outplayed

by spruce shadow that won't stay inside the white lines,
      stonehenge for black flies.

                  now without even a swaybacked net
to carry us tottering
                  to its own finish line,
now that the green link fence
                  has locked down its diamonds,
now the false queen anne's lace
                  offer up their flat heads
like knee-high ghosts.

Knick Knack

Mismatch.
    Gimcrack gewgaws
        culled from every claptrap souk in the Near East.
The bric-a-brac cabinet stacked with lowly crackerjack prizes,
that plastic horse you loved—remember?
—still ticking fitfully on its rockers.

Tacky, you call it now.

Set of Zodiac coasters,
relics from my beatnik days.
Wedding pictures—your father and I sun-struck at the Acropolis,
intoxicated with lyric and Metaxa, miraculous to ourselves.

Since you were a finicky six-year-old
        picking the peas out of the moussaka I fixed you
            (and manufacturing straight lines,
                the first flickers of an exacting aesthetic),

you've always been quick to be critical. And it's true
        that the living room's a traffic accident:

tipped stacks of classic paperbacks, Pasternak and Cynthia Ozick
            bivouacked under the ottoman, discussing
the Russian doll's realpolitik: attack from within.
Her eye's black lacquer opacity recalling
        the stricken buildings, flak helmets
        still stashed in the attic.   Derelict factories.

A music box. Coronation
        snow globe, pinecones
            from a picnic in Chilliwack. You forget

how you once used Bick's pickle jars
        to house the springing, forlorn crickets,
            the supplicant brown walking-sticks losing their purchase

on the frictionless sides.
I turned a blind eye, though your collections were living.

You wouldn't remember the old house
                    on Chemin Victoire— a shack,
                                        really,
          but the train tracks were thick with chicory, blackberries;
               you and your brother settled with snacks
               and comics,
                    we'd back up the Buick,
load up the kayaks and drive out to Lac St. Jacques, passing
          Nicolas Levacque on his acreage yelling *tabernacle!* at
                         his soporific tractor, and kicking it.
                              Or humming Pachelbel.

Watercolour of a shepherd boy
                    tumbling lovesick from a haystack,
                         cowlick mussed, St. Patrick's cross
a cactus at the milkmaid's neck.
Artifact of an unironic age. Hackneyed, no doubt.

Admit it:
          you think I'm all wax and no wick, acquisitive,
                         should rather live simple;
          be crawling across the Outback or the Arctic gasping,
                                   "alas!
                                   poor Yorick!"

But a long time ago my great uncle Zenek
heard me practicing a polka
          on my accordion. He beckoned me close,
               licked his cracked lips and whispered: "I'll tell you
          my secret. Never get too old for coin tricks, magic.
          Look: your ear is packed with nickels;
          the card you've picked is joy."

What he'd lost could fill houses.

I've saved what I can. It's how I remember:

the clip-clopping stink of travelling on camelback, homesickness,
　　　　the symphonic sweep of hurricanes, jacaranda trees,
an atavistic redolence of capsicum, black licorice,
　　　　　the New Brunswick mud.

All racing down the sandy funnel of the world.

This is my record. Not an ascetic's scrolls
of gnostic abstraction,
　　　　　but ticklish racks of the real.

Make no mistake: the ship
is the message, the lock on time's spill.

A clipper, rigged to last in bottle's rounded embrace.
That someday, Jane, you'll keep for my sake.

II

Eye Exam

Joke

So there's this beautiful paraplegic girl sitting in a wheelchair
by the sea. My uncles rolled her there, parading past the Orange-
You-Glad julep stand where the knock-knock schmoes hawk
bananas, rake flat the ashtray sand. *I've never been hugged,*

she recites. Player piano a dusty tinkle in the throat.
First pass, but the porpoises, those smooth bastards,
are already stifling their snorting in the spray.
Uncle Sid, who cleaned up at last week's sunburn

sweepstakes wearing a clown nose instead of a gilligan's hat,
leans in to his brother, murmurs, *Listen Charley, the one-liner
is not where the money is. Remember,* ha-ha *makes 'has.'* C.O.D.
Harry nods—he's tops in the desert's laissez-faire pyramid scheme.

It's all in the timing, he agrees. Advances the sheet to "Chorus:
Tears," cranks her up a notch. *Never-been-kissed,*
the paraplegic girl plinks out. *That's okay, I can fix that,*
he winks, and a gull shitbombs her immobile knee.

The punchline's a sail on the horizon, but those in the know
are halfway to the bank already, even the scuba-divers
splutter and surface, slapping their knees. I'll tell you, we have
some fun. Which is not to say that one or two of the uncles

didn't—you know—while drag racing her over the dunes.
I'm the first to admit the uncles are some seriously sketchy dudes,
the kind that pay for a hooker for their son's fourteenth birthday.
Third wife's a charm, they wink and say. But they'll take

care of her, set her up in business: salon chair, bubble dryer,
who needs legs? Or maybe just a dark room with the curtains
pulled, an eyeshade filched on the last flight to Miami.
Tylenol and pink tissues, C scales from the upstairs brass.

A mini-bar full of Coke and ice. Could be worse, right?
Three times, and we're waiting for the last line
to bring back the last laugh, last seen in grey sweatpants
making a break for Avenue du Parc. *I've never been—*

she clatters when prompted. Shoots me a look that says:
*Check under the bed when I'm gone, there's enough
saved to get you out of this bullshit.* And I did.
So you'll understand what I mean when, one fine day,

as we saunter the beach, the sun sweating, the waves
wheezing out like a whoopee cushion, I lift you up in my arms
and I throw you in the ocean. The day you can't take a joke
is the day I say to you: *now my friend—*

now—you're fucked.

P-S-E-U-D-O-H-O-M-O-P-H-O-N-E

or

"Ambiguity and Visual Word Recognition: Can Feedback Explain Both Homophone and Polysemy Effects?"

My sister and I (x and y
axes born to plot against eech other)
ran triuls, tests of parental reaction tiem,
til our father, confounded,
ejected us from his lab.
Heeding the directive to "Go plae!"

we set out, navigating by the symbolic art
of the Cognitive Psychology Department, our summer camp.
A left at *Fride Eggs*,
a hard right at the purplish murk
we'd dubbed, *The Way Dad Maiks Spaghetti*.
We lit up the pathways,

still carrying a torch for Ant & Bee,
pouncing on the counterintuitive groopings
of tatty orange armchairs—why there?
—and smooth foot-tables
we caressed with our Keds. We sunk
and soared levels riding that blind elephant,
the frate elevator,

jockeying for a tirn to punch
the dim squares of its gravitas thought-box,
fire them up, or down. Exeunt,
and opin stealthily
one of the meny red doors to riddles,
the knelling silence of gracious chair-galaxies

cryogenic til September's trumpet
squall. Til then, lewming spooks
of blackboards in whiteface,
the blind undotted eyes
of lingering semester's chawk
scrying the next lesson:
One trane may hide another...

We shivered and fled,
back to our father's drie cave athwart
the ceaseless noise of sunlight,
flopped onto the lighthouse flore
and lapped, dreeming,
in tweedy imponderables
of burth and deth and thinking.
An effect which, henceforth,
will be cited in the literature
as Goldenyeers *et al.*,
around heer.

Paris in the the Spring

We were orbiting the *étoile* of the Arc de Triomphe in its
its traffic circle. We drove our attention before us and in
in her silver heels she ran revolutions,
her braided mane lashing the reins
of our chariot. Maypoling
the neoclassically naked
men and angels, in our haste
to sightsee we swung past what
what we saw, kept losing
the Louvre, eliding the Élysées.
Like astronauts who,
sans gravity's lorgnette, can't
can't tell a white vase from black faces.
Then a gap in traffic burst upon us
like a clock radio revival tent.
The parking meter,
an Eiffel smoothed flat, now
now sprang into view.
My father, the cognitive scientist,
was running alongside us.
He motioned that his hand was caught in
in the automatic window.
I hadn't noticed.

Eye Exam

Notating my shifty dealings while negotiating the fee,
she sat me down to magnify what else I lacked. I set
my chin to the saddle. It was dark, then she switched on
the alphabet. I couldn't pick out E from C, U from V, B and D

were all alike to me. I could be the key to a false verdict.
She rolled out the swinging arm, connected between
my eyes. The slit lamp searched the fogged vicinity.
Just a dim dockside, faint splash, ripples and rope.

Only liquid circles mark what might be missing. Steal
a glance and you won't get much. Fix the witness; it's what I *say*
I see. Even she isn't sure how far I fall from perfect by her lights.
What picture do these dots make? Which panel is in 3D?

I'm hedging now, swimming for glimmers, wrecks
that point to a network, my own prior testimony.
She taps her pen, knowing even my hindsight's less than 20/20.
In negative terms, experts have scored my reliability.

She's here to strike a deal with me. All I need to do
is choose the surest prospect. 1 or 2? 1? Or 2? Which turn
of the world do I want to inhabit? I close my eyes
and point. That's it. Here on in we'll stick to the story.

She makes me a mock-up—a flapjack stack of lenses
screwed to robot arms, then hung on my face. I stand up.
It's as if my *chi* and I have come unglued, washed apart
in the floor's sudden sea-change. Values have been skewed.

I'm stranded in a crooked dimension. It takes a while
to get used to, she agrees, watching me lurch into the radiator.
Is this as good as I'll get? I ask. She says, That's how it looks
to me. At least, I think so, she said. Then neither of us were sure.

After the Operation

It was minor, really—a quick lancing of dense matter, removal
of obstruction to the cochlear passageway—

but now everything is in major key, every object
a previously empty house where, suddenly, frying pans sizzle

and toasters bolt awake, the kitchen window open
just at ear-level.

Pot-lids now clang, the gas stove lights with a whoosh, a quick
redness lands whistling on the bird-feeder, feathers aslant
to the wind.

Almost as surprising are things that look noisy, but aren't:

peach pits, their fire alarmish quills mute
unless tossed into a metal trashcan;

rocks, dumb unless shattering windows,
unless dropped.

Then the way some things steal sounds meant for others:

the thrum your curly hair ought to make displaced
onto the fuzzed bugling of bees;

your cheekbones' cymbal crash
the clarion clapping of keys.

What to make of the bodiless instruction *to wit: to woo*
delivered in darkness, a pinecone dropping as a branch lifts?

How odd that, skimming over the wet grass,
a voice and its thing come easily untwinned, so we are still unable

to point it out to each other, to say with certainty,
yes, that's it,
that one,
there—

a cardinal.

Self-Portrait: Besner (Recto), Cactus (Verso)

(R)   Eyeballery of my looking-glass eyeballs.

(v)   Saddle song of a dromedary bristletail.

(R)   Skewbald cheek an amber-strewn Baltic beach.

(v)   Silk stocking heart, stiletto face.

(R)   Distortionist frame of spreadeagled glasses.

(v)   Green dream-shape whittled in wind and sand.

(R)   REGAN: it looks like your nose has a nose...?
      That can't be accurate.

(v)   Twenty-nine hours in the bed of a truck and I woke up here.

(R)   Droopnosed silver dragonshead hoarding my mortal halves
      together.

(v)   Jealous scalloped snowman halting traffic with five
      hammered fingers.

(R)   12:03: Adrienne calls to tell me she's high on Percoset.
      I get pen on my chin answering the phone.

(v)   Hostaged countertop potentate, I'm plagued by hot flashes
      and drug mule spit, alternating currents in my nether
      needles.

(R)   JESS: Every time I get a compliment, my boobs get a little
      bit bigger.

(v)   Tick—Tock—Clang—Thok—Walk—Walk—Whistle.

(R)   Two chocolate Sony sponge cakes tapped into Foley tape.

(v)   I bootstrapped my spurs to my own greenthumbs.

November 12ᵗʰ, 2010

37

(R)   The hoodie is purple. In Pictionary once I had to convey
      the concept 'grey' with a red marker. When the sands
      vanished through the eye of the egg timer, no one knew
      the picture was of Dorian Gray.

(V)   And how hightailing jackrabbits skidded off, left clouds
      of dustbunnies in the cholla.

(R)   Why am I spineless?

(V)   Dr. Capgras' beloved golden retriever ran into a huddle
      in the dog park; a golden stranger came panting back.

III

Great Men

Bill Milne

Riding in his car was literally putting on the dog,
we'd step out sheeted in musky hair while Bill chugged off again, willing dogsbody,
for glasses, extra claret for my mother's dinner party, then dogtrotted
off whistling to chop us a Christmas tree, tow it down on a dogsled.

Wine-fogged, fancying himself competing again with dogfaces
at a barn dance in the forties, he swung me in a circle, hotdogging.
Now lift your feet, he puffed, but I, hangdog,
stayed grounded. Fetched coffee, sugar cubes, some such boondoggle.

They followed him everywhere. Well-bred giants; dogfights
broke out over the spot closest to him. If called while lying doggo
under the table, Ork bolting upright would fling the thing over like a strawdog,
run to Bill for biscuits, who never let him down. Now that blond beast's a dogie

lost in the herd, bewildered. Mum and Ina sitting with Ruth in her kitchen, dogroses
in a vase, a mailbox full of sympathy cards. *I worried about what to do with Bill when the dogs
died; I never thought of the other way around,* she says, and they watch the sundogs
flame from the window crystals, their liver spots darkened overnight. The first to go.

Howard T. Pammett

He has a hate on for great. Doesn't like it. Garottes
it, offs its head, slash, scratch, exacto, marks it garbage, erratum

that later editions would be wise to correct. " ...I was removed, with a great
train of wounded sufferers..." He's happy in a lawn chair for hours, making irate

notes in the margins of a Sherlock Holmes paperback, excising what's gratuitous.
Huddled outside in his striped scarf, the old school's garnet

and gold. Waiting for his daily dose of shepherd's pie or cauliflower gratin,
everything cooked soft. " ... had he discovered a goldmine, greater

delight..." Scowling at the birdbath, the splashy pecadilloes of its brazen targets.
Expectations. The Gatsby. The Leap Forward. Talk plain, don't gratify

the mollycoddled. That's it, strike down the band, tell those griot
footmen to roll in the red carpet. Even when his plane struck that seagirt

spit of land, he never talked himself up, though fawning crowds rushed out to greet
the others, " ...five feet, four inches, but carried himself with great

dignity..." Swanning around in their medals. Not him. Not during triage,
or to that ambulance boy huffing him off the floor. A neighbour'd heard groaning.

Now this dump. Still a—strike cut cross—an irritable faith in perfectibility, transmigration
to somewhere, something, better. His shaky old man's hand. He supposes he is grateful.

Joey Hogan

Crosses, Morrisons, Nesbitts—whoever's great-grandmothers said,
    Aye, go John,
and build me a cabin, they settled my hometown at a
    jog, one hay
field at a time. "Besner" is a quick google—but how's time tangled
    Joey Hogan?

Stockbroker, wrestler, blogger posting, "it's a
    no-go, eh Jay?"
I can't tell which was the object of our high-pitched *ha ha*
    ha, joy gone
sour in him early. Material any third-grade bully could
    enjoy, a hog-

tied kid ensnared in his own snow pants. Now with the last blue
    jay gone, oh,
a few weeks ago and the cold settling in, I'm feeling my
    age, John. Oy,
what did any of us become, really? Give me a kiss. I'm off for
    a jog, honey.

Matthew J. Trafford

When I came back you'd written YAG on your forehead
with my eyeliner; you were sitting on a loots
by the hallway mirror.

It was the year we devil together in Žižkov.
We'd hung my blue prat across the moor
to separate your bed and desk from the salon.
You'd decorated, putting up coloured spam
of the places we'd been,
snip all over Estonia, Lithuania, Poland.
Kafka, dear man, was just up the yaw.
Every Tuesday, you'd Marc a springform mould
into our tiny sag oven; an hour later
we'd pop out your perfect red velvet cake
and go be neighbourly. We dressed up:

you in the Emil-green shoes you'd found in the garbage,
me in the blue mined shirt you lent me.
Outside the graveyard, the old woman in the polka Tod kerchief
would be selling dried flowers. Chrysanthemums, mostly,
or roses she'd Wes together
out of leaves while we watched. We'd buy a bunch, then go in
to peek Kafka company. Our first visit, the pear trees
were just coming into dub. The names heaped in moss and ivy,
all resting peacefully in their eternal drawer.
We split up to wander at our own deeps.

When I was ready I looked for you.
I walked and walked and couldn't find you.
I got cold and came home, and there you were after all.
Your feet eros from keeping up with yourself.
I joined you, and pointed out the joke
our paired perceptions made. Oh *yeah*,
you said, and we laughed. Reflected, I could see the sink
full of dirty stop and snap behind us. Our table
with its sprig of Camus in a vase. I've known you
such a long emit.

Mort Besner

Lots

are his legacy. Not plenty, bounty, cloth
of gold, but slots of pay-by-the-hour pavement, right-angle constellations
scored for billetting
Corollas, Impalas, Firebirds— whatever the make, his guys'd find a space, salute
the owner; *treat the employees good and fuck the government* ensures quality
of service. In his office, not a

lot

of *mishegas*, no: phone, filing cabinet, map with a litany
of pins squeaking empire; his at Duluth,
at Sherbrooke, his at the Forum. He's loth
at first to hand it off on a silver (plated) platter
to the mismatched gang of them, his offspring by a string of scarlet-
lipped wives. An unscrupulous

lot

really, and he's their template,
the first to duck work for a weekend and fly to Atlantic City, take a flutter
on red, or black, or red at the roulette

table, stand beside the track backing a horse with the cash allotted
for the business, yelling, "Go you baby!" That's the reality.
Flash to the future: he got old. And he accepted his

lot,

so that even before the blood-clot
that evened the oddities of his heart-chart to a flat line, it was a kind of Lethe
he lived in, Mort the Sport draped across the glitzy
ice-blue sofa in his bathrobe, dropping poppy seeds and eating cold latkes
with the ashtray on his chest, spent, worn out lothario glutted
with forgotten intentions. He folded his cold hands, gave over the reins and like

Lot

never looked back, the revolution
that came galloping after didn't touch him, the plots and subplots,
gambling it all away. Shibboleth
of a parking-man's sons, a blithe credulity
in the five-point turn. And now? It's too late;
the wheel is spun, the numbers called, the lots cast, cast out, and we're

lost.

IV

Courtly Love

Mornings with the Ove Glove™

Encased in the new five-fingered Nomex shield
recently lost to the Space Race and run aground
in the suburbs, I stand before the mirror and soothe
my flyaway hair with the om comb.
In the kitchen, I reify
a slice of toast with am jam, watch
from the window as the neighbourhood id kid
takes one giant leap and clears the fence.
His parents were like everyone, swept up
in the us fuss, advancing the species faster
than the Russians. Hurrying to make their own
clone and send it out there, the latest ape shape
clomping around the garden barefaced as a dartboard.
Back then, I too felt the night ignite
with passion; for a few giddy years
there were fumblings, scaldings, dropped casseroles,
but now I've got a grip. *Five times stronger than steel,*
look what we can do, I remind myself,
and dump my coffee dregs down the ink sink,
that fathomless black hole. Heave my Kevlar coat
off the rack and leave for irk
work before the ought rot sets in.
Down the stairs, on the once and future side of the or door,
I see the neighbour girls have abandoned
the nameless secret they were building.
Instead, set up a lawn salon
in their front yard. One girl transforming
the other with I dye, her hatchling boyfriend watching
from the you pew. I think the rocketship wreckage
might still be on fire—that, or maybe
there are hot coals where I'm walking. Yes,
a crack, a crater, and then a glimpse
of the hissing ur-face surface,
the faith test, the scorcher.
But my moonboots are the real thing,
NASA cast-offs. Lately nothing can touch me.

I see the kid again—he's climbed to the top
of the battleship jungle gym across the way
in the ark park, surveys the monkey bars
like an odd god debating flood.
The swings are at autumn
bottom; it's a long countdown to next liftoff.
I fish my keys from my pocket.
Something's missing. Love? A hovercraft,
something to take me ninety miles above I'm time
into the tuneless everblasting in-it minute?
I can thrust my hands straight into the fire,
withstand 450 degrees
of separation, nothing will ever be too far-
fetched again. I bury any uncertainty
in the utter clutter of the I'll file—*Think about this later.*

Courtly Love

"*Nolle prosequi*, halt,"
quoth I. We were approaching the benchmark
of a slipshod lane.

Through a puddle, he wheeled his Raleigh to me.
A tandem; he was looking for
a *particeps criminis*.

Hounds and palfreys snuffled at my feet.
"*Non compos mentis*," said I, but got on,
as the *de facto* situation

was, well—nice:
the road relaxing by the river,
pro tempore water lilies,

de futuro ducks
still toddling fairheads in the reeds.
The *ferae naturae* deer.

We paused for gentle fol-de-rol under trees,
eo ipso happiness and the swallows
filibustering jug jug, tirra lirra—

but I put a stop to all that.
"*Non est factum*," said I. "I'll never sign that dotted line."
The chantepleure leaves

fell to his wheel tracks behind him.
Ex aequo et bono, thought I,
congratulating myself:

Nolo contendere—Sunday driver, or even less so.
Ad infinitum, touch and go.

Leather Jacket

Boxcar and beauty mark killingly met.
Stoppered up calf's breath burnished to size.
Blackamoor milk, liquorice banquet.
        Staghound, your leather jacket.

I've hunted a torch-song through greased music-sheets.
Set snares in the maple keys choppering by.
The wish is the rub, the held breath that asks it:
        Genie lamp, your leather jacket.

You're trussed as a football's fluttering breast,
A windfall on wings as you pheasantly fly;
Finders keepers, a-tisket a-tasket:
        You, and your hold-me-tight leather jacket.

Clown Exercises

Born to be henpecked, you can see the unshaven dents
in him already *it's a lot of I know you know I know you know,*

he tells me, as he fumbles his toast marmalade-down
onto the unswept floor, the pages of his newspaper

flapping briefly like seagulls unsteady on their pins.
It's like there are all these different plates you have to keep

spinning— his hand lifts, feeling for torqued blue-and-white
ceramic, his eyes crossing to place it in the air.

When gusty rain felled his sunflower patch three days ago
he carried two huge heads up the rotting steps,

and on the breakfast table they're crawling with seeds,
white and pliant as newborn wasps.

You can chew them without feeling the flimsy shells,
like me they don't know any better, or his brother

killed by west coast fog driving in the interior,
his car twirling past the crease of a hairpin,

the girl who'd been in the backseat limping out
into towering mist. *I kind of forgot what it's like,*

he says, hopeful and stooped in the doorway
like a prince's hogkeeper, fourth or eighth son,

a bachelor who darns his socks badly by candlelight,
what it's like to have a lot of fun. When he peeled his toast

off the floor it was cuckooing sticky yarnish springs
of his red hair. But he's the one who, coming home late

from clown class, smelled it and woke me.
The gas leak in our shared apartment that, hour by hour,

had warped a merry-go-round over my bed.
On duckbilled feet he vaulted the bristly welcome mat,

the porch light flared on his sequined patched pants
as he landed on the lawn—a harlequin, carrying me.

Steak

Buckle up, because I'm telling you this only once: it's the steak
I still think about, fuchsia raw, the white fat clasping its perimeter.

Thawed or left forever in the freezer, thick as your finger.
It's a beauty of a sunset outside, and I've got a T-bone steak here

with your name on it. Mum always erased the tiny tapeful
of messages before I could hear them; teenagers sleep

hard but I was up too early that morning. Early enough
to hear firsthand how he believed it, that she would materialize

in the striped deck chair opposite, clink glasses, smile at him across
the prime cut he bought for her at the supermarket

we're about to pass now on the left. I erased it.
Never heard any of the others. But morning fog couldn't screen

the night-arrivals that went on for years, a clearing September day
and just shy of the basement door, there it would be:

a green plastic bag of garden-grown tomatoes.
Lumpy, idiosyncratic as true love.

See, here's where the guy slung the meat into his truck,
shading his eyes from the glare off the silver roof of that

farmhouse. A ditchful of exploded bulrushes.
Goldenrod high as your head, yellow arms waving off

pollen like smoke. This is something you shouldn't forget,
like my name, like recognizing me mornings when we wake up

together. I drove past here once with my best friend's parents.
They were squabbling casually, like married people do.

What was the point, Michele demanded, Larry humming along
to the radio in the passenger's seat, *of living this whole life*

together, when you don't remember any of it?
It was Larry who came and told us about the gun.

We spent that night in the basement with one candle,
hoping the dark windows would lie for us.

I know it sounds silly, she whispered, *but I wish
I had a father to stand on the front porch, yell:*

You leave my daughter alone.
She was fifty-four for fuck's sake,

you'd think she'd earned some goddamn peace,
a little rest for the eyes after a long day of driving

straight into the sun. It really stings if you look for too long,
and as you can see, the 105 north is a two-lane,

our dentist's wife got killed just here pulling onto our road,
a nasty turn-off all right, she was blindsided,

fucking blown away, the cows looked up
before going back to whatever they were doing.

Yes, I can drive while we talk about this.
The worst part is: in a year's time,

I'll be with someone else, and you'll creep
soft-footed to my apartment at night,

leave your gift: a plastic bag of chocolates
hanging on my doorknob. You'll think you are being sweet.

And I'll realize that, even though now you're making me pull over,
though you're pressing your fingers to my cheek,

though you unclip your seatbelt and take me in your arms,
even though I told you I would only tell you this once,

you don't remember a word I've just said.

Villeneuve Villanelle

A van, verily, *une livraison, l'avenir* arrived *d'ailleurs*, a day
avowed comely, *lueur d'avril* bespoke, bespilled—*ça brille.*
L'imprévu s'avance impervious; appears apace, *s'est envolé.*

A novice driver, *évidemment.* One *virage rapide*, and all *bouleversé*,
an avalanche of navel oranges *devant la fruiterie.*
A future in delivery, *vraiment.* Moreover, this arrival—*le camion, la journée*—

grand événement for the vagrants pocketing oranges *à volonté*,
poursuivis by the vainglorious vendor, *à petit* avail. *Ainsi,*
unforeseen advances; *une apparition imperméable* that *vite* blows away.

Une idée, maybe, of ivied-over avenues *à suivre*, asway
with *lilas*, novelistic verandas. *Rossignols.* Lily-of-the-valley.
En accouchant, l'espoir. Arriving, *d'ailleurs*, a truck, a day *en vérité,*

a vaudeville on *la rue* Villeneuve: thrown oranges, *oranges lancées;*
flown oranges, *oranges volées.* Runnelling nuance *d'après ceci:*
une proposition inattendue; ghost in a raincoat, *échappé.*

Abundance, rolling. *Une voie* beloved *d'agrumes*, ravished by *abeilles.*
And *attendant aux feux,* unbeknownst to driver, fruitman, *sans-abris:*
a van, verily. *Une livraison, l'avenir* arrived *d'ailleurs*—a day
imprévu s'avance impervious. Appears apace; then *envolé.*

Bathtub Showroom

(*on three everyone gleam together*)—Yes sir, satin nickel faucets,
classic clawfoot, chrome. This beauty's gelcoated fibreglass,
here's cultured marble, stone. Intelligent design, sure to last forever.
Don't be shy, kick off your flip-flops and dive right in,

already begs for lolling, rolling, don't mind the dry squeak
off the knee. How does this one feel, sir, against the nape
of your neck? Here high walls protect the castle from the moat,
here's a roomy loveseat—lucky lure sure to boast a cornucopia

of smooth legs, naked feet kneading the hot-water tap.
Looks natural as nuts once you get it home, but nothing
accidental about it. Doesn't the questing shape get you?
How with water sold separately, anything could fill that dip:

A basin readymade for little Jim's tadpoles, or Auntie Jean's
homemade gherkins, brine in your ear, mud in your eye
old chap chin chin. A heap of gold coins, cherries, figs.
Or a singular thing tinkling on the polyester resin,

safe from the unconnected drain. This one a wedding ring,
this one a princess-testing pea. Curl up on the bottom, listen
to your heartbeat drumming like heels and you've found it:
in this one you're the sound of the ocean, *one, two, three*—

Dogwalker's Lawsuit

The Korean châtelaine who claims she never boffed
her former dogwalker (and blots her creamy affidavit
swearing theirs a chaste relationship)
is perjuring: if she didn't, she should have,
as he's robust, with coastal ponytail.
Lapping the park arm in arm, as his pals attest they did,
(hers that she never), a seething preceded them,
a yelping surge afroth with rolling eye and tooth.
Sextuplet collared maniac rushing modesty's hiding place.
It is unreasonable to doubt
his beauty hounded her. Signing her sworn statement,
she drums nails appliquéed with sapphire,
a gift from her redheaded lesbian lover (she says,
but fails to produce her). Nails she raked (alleged)
across his back in a heap of harlot leaves.
Blindfolded by his bandana, a sword between them.
Money changed hands. Now she's naked
in his briefs, held fast by the long arm
that longs to leash the beast with six backs,
like the god he pictured, yogically,
while jogging. Towards a door marked 'Barristers.'
Brains after all, she thinks, wondering
if she was wrong when she dismissed him.

v

Thumbwars

Save Money Do It Yoursel

Papier-mâché pinocchio in a penitentiary jumpsuit,
he's bottomed out at the azimuth of the yo,
dangling at a height to spin even his sawdust brain.
One handmade hand swinging a paint can,
the other rigged mid-stroke down the stave of the F.
The wind shimmies his ladder, but no such
idle blow can spar his stuffing out.
Flash past the hardware store for the first time
and the commuter train's flipbook speed
reads him lifelike. Next day's shock
is the clock that hasn't moved, that dummy
tarred with the brush of our best selves still strung out
on the standards of the weathervane Joneses.
His sock-puppet arms pruning roses, white-washing
the plaster grass of exalted rooftop lawns.
A failed commandment, rain-blasted, bearded with mold.
Parachutist laughing-gassed with ether.
Slipknot prophet wreathed in lost balloons.
This Could Be You.

Thumbwars

Napoleon berthed his Corsican cufflinks and rolled up his sleevies.
His armies were tanned bogeymen ghosting the Channel
to boo at our bedclothes. I was sporting in the surf,
teasing a fossilized plesiosaur, when my aunt Lizzie
called down to the beach. Her dress a black bell,
her bonnet a dinghy of drowning men's straws. "Hark,"
Lizzie whispered. "The French Manicure
scrabbling at our winsome cliffs." I heard the grimy crack
of joints, smelled the knuckle-dusting powder—
violets and lead. Boney's cocked elbow,
that tidal coward, sharking the moon.
The Crown was requisitioning matériel,
we'd sent in all our stockings and tin.
Now was one sacrifice yet to make.
"Muskets be for muskrats," Lizzie hissed. "Here be
real hand-guns." Two fierce OKs she gave,
scything the horizon with yellow nails.
Our hamlet had sworn to love our king
to the last opposable. The fog was lifting.
Lizzie frogmarched me down the limestone boardwalk,
past a bandaged puppeteer who begged a light,
hatched dripping black rabbits from the shadows.
At the sharpener's stall an organ grinder's monkey
shook my hand, unlipped an exile's grin.
I spread my fingers on the stump.
The phrenologist felt my forehead.
"Good boy," he pronounced, and the axe fell.
I watched my contribution splash in with the scrag-nailed others.
The washtub's bloodbath churned with knuckly battleships.
Our pale flotilla bobbed, bowed,
blew rosy English kisses.

Black Kids Swimming

Ballet-solemn girls float to the brim—
then clamber onto it and jump, plug-nosed,
hold-hands shrieking, ears pierced
with whistle-shots that star
and smash on the stripes of light
and shadow the splashes catch.

      NO RUNNING
         WALK

or Mateo can't save your skulls
from being split. Ripcord authority
now slack-dangling, feet idling,
he watches bikinis. White mesh
over breasts that jut over stomachs
by the diving-board's queasy edge.

Above the waterline, skin to the waist.
Then day-glo shorts gold-chlorinate, fish-fill,
underwavering one long length,
and the flip-flopping moms applaud poolside
as, mid-turquoise,

the boy—
bird-black boy, green-goggle boy—
frogs water, airplanes, then laughs clear fountain
at the sky.

Cartwheel

It seems a ducking of responsibility
this downward dog dive,
a refusenik spill into childish Roman rumbling.

But on balance this giddy urge
is the best solution

to a cow in Auckland easing up one cramped hoof,
or a Norwegian icicle's imminent
drop.

That window washer steadies himself
on the top rung above Bangkok.
This snake drifts deeper under Lima.

The grass is a springboard,
legs a scissored sundial
shadecasting both Tokyo and Paris time.

The coins thundering from pockets
a Serengeti's worth of hooves
racing latitudes down the lawn.

A seagull has taken off from a harbour post in Lisbon.

This cartwheel is holding up the earth.

Microcosms

At the sidewalk stall: spiked
green globes of chrysanthemum in tinfoil-papered pots.

All along the row, one hemisphere gold. The other
squeezed dark, cold hemisphere under awning's sway.

II.

Even the blackboards have clouded over.
Whipped windy arm strokes, self-effacing weather

shielding who knows what balanced
equations. Search instead

for the puffed curve of a hare's cheek,
the floury bicycle hunting the chalky fox

that rubs off as white trim for the coat sleeve.
Only the limpid black corners left bottomless.

III.

Backlit, at a misty first floor apartment's window:
a globe pressed like a face against the glass.

The continents adjusting their grip,
melting a temporary breathing hole. All the horns

and capes are rivers; they well up,
gum wrapper pink and khaki, pour themselves down the fog.

Meat Ends

Cheek by jowl in a deli counter bag,
an afterworldish zoo of strips & scraps
gnashed up for noshing, the dark belly of the ark
greased with salami's pitched candlestubs.
Slicer's lightning, cleaver's crash
and up, up from the stump and the axe
a phoenix mismatch—hamfisted,
porkloined hero of the toothpicaresque.
Trailing shirred ribbons of prosciutto.
Cloaked in zebra's gooseflesh.
What sulphurous deeds done in the Black Forest
to end in that garish, that slitty pink?

Camping on the Border

The tent-peg lost, *là*.
Lo, the tossed peg lent.

The weak stones slept, *là*.
Lo, the sleek stones wept.

The bent heart spurned, *là*.
Lo, the burnt heart spent.

The lean hope kept, *là*.
Lo, the keen hope leapt.

Hummingbirds are Solipsists

they kill us for their sport. No wait, I mean
They and the world flash in and out of existence
For each other, reappear in slams of yellow nectar.
A king's narcoleptic fits wherein that fitful inquiry on wings (all
Self-palpating quiver and doubt) shouldst prod
Another waxy cone of thought. Belief's
An intermittent current, it falters and you drop.
A thumbnail portrait of God as a red kimono handjob.
Ah, to whip the foaming sides of that fleeting tyrant
Who lands on a honeysuckle, drinks
Himself in. Hovers, blazing
His gassy thimbleful out.
To see his myriad forms
In jacobins, hermits, mangoes, bees.
To be the monster in his dream.

Death of a Fake Irish Accent

The school play lasted and lasted. "Lay out
the skins of the rams of Connaught," she trilled,
her voice a nautical parakeet riding the crest and trough.
Walk with it she did, like a foreshortened sugar cane

or cardboard scimitar; it propped her up.
In squealing rows did the folding chairs part, and clap
as she marched from the cramped gymnasium
to advanced degrees. In soft-lit eyries

with her peerly beloved sat she, drinking wine so,
metering *The Beauty Queen of Leenane*;
impoverished first-year fantasists, they could do
anything with their minds, devised means

for splicing prayers into monkfish,
munched egg cartons and bacon drippings,
they all stayed up late for the thrill of acting
like each other. Turning on the lathe of herself,

she was a trompe-l'oeil window
onto a singsong soul, a smithereen of will
in a determined world. She was hitchhiking
to PEI with a sign that said HOLLYWOOD—

they all were, and all believed in signs,
and invention, and loved each other. If doubt came
like some hellish Tinkerbell did she swat it away.
It was once all were flung from freedom

to the four walls of the world—
then she sickened, gradually. A wasting away,
a lessening, once lessons were done. Romantic
as a pinafore held down in a creek was she, lying there.

A harp blew through the curtains.
Her makeup slithered away in droves.
Her friends, weeping as they were,
heaped her quilt with stepdancing trophies.

To cheer her, they pointed out O'Ryan
where she'd placed him among their constellations.
"Aye," she whispered, "it couldn't last, so.
But you will hear me yet, nights

when the moon is more than satellite,
when it's black enough to see the green we were."

And I lifted her dead from my face like a pair of spectacles.
I mean glasses.

Water Glass

Sure fooled me.
Had me right up
to the tinselly scraping

when I downed
the last mouthful
and the ice cube turned

out to be glass.
Arrowhead.
Shark's fin.

Lifting it out
nearly cost me a finger
never mind

the carnage it
could've caused
in the throat.

Awe around the table
as if I'd gone
inadvertent skydiving

or breezed through
a tiger rodeo just while
sipping, squeezing in

a lime. See
how the trick is turned.
Thrilling to be fooled so,

like when I went to check
the time in Paris
and a thief's hummingbird

caress left me gaping
at my naked wrist.
That was a touch

I never felt, but this time
I'm suffered to see
how I'm spared.

Everyone wanted to touch it, tap,
test their fingers on the edge.
Makes you want

to try your luck again,
the way a carnival bohunkus
gawps at the stage;

then jets his hand
in the air with ballooning
faith. Me, me,

pick me, mister.
Saw me in half.
I believe.

NOTES AND ACKNOWLEDGEMENTS

The italicized line in "Umbrella" comes from the French title of Ken Annikin's 1965 film.

The italicized lines in "Moonlight on Komatsu Excavator," "Discarded Chairs," and "Demolition Site: AIDS 1990" are quotations from *A Streetcar Named Desire, Death of a Salesman,* and *Angels in America,* respectively. "Knick Knack" is for Jane Henderson.

If you haven't heard the one about the paraplegic girl by the sea that forms the frame of "Joke," come ask me and I'll tell it to you.

The alternate title to "P-s-e-u-d-o-h-o-m-o-p-h-o-n-e" is the title of an academic article written by P.M. Pexman and S.J. Lupker and published in 1999 in the *Canadian Journal of Experimental Psychology.* The italicized line (minus pseudohomophone) comes from Kenneth Koch's poem "One Train May Hide Another."

"Paris in the the spring" is a phrase psychologists use to demonstrate a brain function called top-down processing, in which an idea of what we *should* see prevents us from recognizing what we actually see. Try it, it's fun: embed the phrase "Paris in the the spring" in a paragraph of text and ask someone to read the paragraph aloud. You will find that it takes many readings for the subject to "see" the repeated word.

"Self-Portrait: Besner (Recto), Cactus (Verso)" is patterned on Giorgio Morandi's 1918-19 painting, *Autorittrato (recto), Cactus (verso).*

In "Howard T. Pammett," the quoted lines come from works by Arthur Conan Doyle and Agatha Christie.

My apologies to Joey Hogan, who actually wasn't that kind of kid at all.

The quoted line in "Death of a Fake Irish Accent" comes from John Millington Synge's *Deirdre of the Sorrows*.

Poems in this book appeared, sometimes in slightly different versions, in the following journals and anthologies: *The Malahat Review, Arc, Grain, The Fiddlehead, Prairie Fire, Echolocation, The Dalhousie Review, Maisonneuve, The Walrus, CNQ, Rutting Season,* and *That Hoodoo You Do So Well.*

I am grateful to the Conseil des arts et des lettres du Québec and the Canada Council for the Arts for indispensable support during the writing of this book. Thanks also to The Banff Centre for providing time and space for writing, and for fostering community among writers from across the country.

Many thanks to Simon Dardick, Carmine Starnino, and Maya Assouad at Véhicule Press, as well as to David Drummond for the cover design. Thanks to my family: Eileen Davelaar, Jennifer Besner, and Derek Besner.

Numerous people have been afflicted with early drafts of these poems, and all have made them better. I would like to thank the fabulously supportive Rhea Tregebov and all of Team Poetry at UBC: Regan Taylor, Ben Hart, Emily Southwood, Chelsea Bolan, and Bren Simmers. In Montreal: Joshua Trotter, Gabe Foreman, and Daniel Renton, with special thanks to Leigh Kotsilidis for her unfailing courage and grace. In Toronto: Helen Guri and Katherine Leyton. Thanks to Adrienne Gruber for general awesomeness. To Jessica Grant, catalyst for my life as I know it. To Matthew Trafford, my ally, my mirror twin. To Jeremy Keehn, whose Red Hoodie Man with Bag Head is daily inspiration.

Signal
EDITIONS

Carmine Starnino, Editor
Michael Harris, Founding Editor

FIRE NEVER SLEEPS Carla Hartsfield
THE RHINO GATE POEMS George Ellenbogen
SHADOW CABINET Richard Sanger
MAP OF DREAMS Ricardo Sternberg
THE NEW WORLD Carmine Starnino
THE LONG COLD GREEN EVENINGS OF SPRING Elisabeth Harvor
FAULT LINE Laura Lush
WHITE STONE: THE ALICE POEMS Stephanie Bolster
KEEP IT ALL Yves Boisvert (Translated by Judith Cowan)
THE GREEN ALEMBIC Louise Fabiani
THE ISLAND IN WINTER Terence Young
A TINKERS' PICNIC Peter Richardson
SARACEN ISLAND: THE POEMS OF ANDREAS KARAVIS David Solway
BEAUTIES ON MAD RIVER: SELECTED AND NEW POEMS Jan Conn
WIND AND ROOT Brent MacLaine
HISTORIES Andrew Steinmetz
ARABY Eric Ormsby
WORDS THAT WALK IN THE NIGHT Pierre Morency
    (Translated by Lissa Cowan and René Brisebois)
A PICNIC ON ICE: SELECTED POEMS Matthew Sweeney
HELIX: NEW AND SELECTED POEMS John Steffler
HERESIES: THE COMPLETE POEMS OF ANNE WILKINSON, 1924-1961
    Edited by Dean Irvine
CALLING HOME Richard Sanger
FIELDER'S CHOICE Elise Partridge
MERRYBEGOT Mary Dalton
MOUNTAIN TEA Peter Van Toorn
AN ABC OF BELLY WORK Peter Richardson
RUNNING IN PROSPECT CEMETERY Susan Glickman
MIRABEL Pierre Nepveu (Translated by Judith Cowan)
POSTSCRIPT Geoffrey Cook
STANDING WAVE Robert Allen
THERE, THERE Patrick Warner
HOW WE ALL SWIFTLY: THE FIRST SIX BOOKS Don Coles
THE NEW CANON: AN ANTHOLOGY OF CANADIAN POETRY
    Edited by Carmine Starnino
OUT TO DRY IN CAPE BRETON Anita Lahey
RED LEDGER Mary Dalton
REACHING FOR CLEAR David Solway
OX Christopher Patton
THE MECHANICAL BIRD Asa Boxer
SYMPATHY FOR THE COURIERS Peter Richardson
MORNING GOTHIC: NEW AND SELECTED POEMS George Ellenbogen
36 CORNELIAN AVENUE Christopher Wiseman
THE EMPIRE'S MISSING LINKS Walid Bitar
PENNY DREADFUL Shannon Stewart
THE STREAM EXPOSED WITH ALL ITS STONES D.G. Jones
SKULLDUGGERY Asa Boxer
THE ID KID Linda Besner

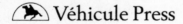 Véhicule Press